Petals

A LOVE BOOK OF POEMS

ANDREW
VITALIS

Prairie Pond
PUBLISHING

Printed and bound in the United States of America

First Printing, January 2022

ISBN 978-0-9968968-7-0

First Edition

Editor: Debra Jacobson
Cover & Layout Design: Ashley Sarauer

Published by Prairie Pond Publishing
New Richmond, Wisconsin 54017, USA
www.PrairiePondPublishing.com

If my days are running out,

I am at peace.

I want you to know you have set me free.

For one who is supposed to come up with the

right words to explain what I mean, when it

comes to explaining how I feel about you,

the words escape me.

I love you with everything I have;

everything that is inside of me.

I hope these words give you some

idea of what I mean.

How you are my everything –

The woman of my dreams.

Preface

As I sit here, I am almost paralyzed with fear. Fear that once I finish this narrative and push send, there is no going back. This is official. This is real. This book of poems is now out there for everyone to see.

Everyone.

Fear that I will be judged by my family. My friends. My community. Fear that I will be attacked and looked down upon by friend and strangers alike. And then there is my "other family"- the numerous cops who I have met throughout the years who might see me as being weak. After all, cops are supposed to be macho. Cops are supposed to hide their emotions and keep them bottled up inside... from *everyone*. They are not supposed to talk like this!

Fear that my kids will read this and think that these poems were meant to be critical of their mom, my first wife, when in reality it has nothing to do with her or my "prior life." The truth is and what I have realized through this journey is that I wasn't ready to love back then- to TRULY love during my first marriage. I had to be broken down to see life differently. I had to realize that I was not in control; God was. I had to learn what perspective meant, how to be grateful, to lead with respect and give myself fully to something bigger than myself. We both failed. If not for being broken down into puzzle pieces, I would have never learned how to complete the picture.

My current wife, my best friend, we talk about the subject of these poems often. We both admit that if we had met at some other point prior in our lives, when both of us thought we knew what life was all about, we would have never made it. We simply weren't ready to see and appreciate the absolute power the other one possessed. We were not ready to take in and appreciate the beauty of life. Perspective. Appreciation. Respect. Love.

I have been asked from time to time why I decided to write this book, and even more than that, why go through the process of publishing it and opening myself up to the negative feedback, thoughts and anxiety that will no doubt come from time to time. Let's be honest - these poems are not for everyone. I do believe however with every ounce of my soul that this book is right for the "right" person.

The "right" couple.

The "right" situation, at just the right time.

Maybe these poems are the words a husband wishes to share with his wife; words that he feels and wants to say but can't always seem to find the words. Maybe they are words shared by newlyweds who have found love and their passion for one another makes them feel like they are continuing to see one another for the first time - over and over again. Maybe these narratives will remind someone that their spouse or romantic partner represent exactly what the poems say and it's precisely how they feel; they just forgot and it's time to remember again. Maybe the words will strike a cord with someone who is searching for their soulmate and the poems are a reminder that their angel could be, and is, right around the corner. Maybe the meaning behind the words represent hope for that person who is broken and hurting; knowing that someday very soon those storm clouds will clear and the sun will once again shine. It did for me.

This book is my proof that God's hand is powerful you just need to stop, listen and embrace what's in front of you; even when your heart seemingly can't take anymore. Especially when your heart is bleeding and tired. Those days when your fear of what might happen outweighs the possibility of what can.

I hope.

In the end, I have always told my children that fear cannot, and should not, control us. If you believe in something embrace it with everything you have. I honestly feel that I have a duty to share my journey with others. Maybe the best way to describe it is this: I feel as though I have a divine responsibility to give back and this is the best way I know how to do it. While scared about what may come of this, my duty to help outweighs that fear - it needs to. At the end of the day I can only hope that this book will help you find, re-connect with (if needed) and recognize the love in our life. While doing so, find your true self in the process.

It's funny because my entire life I always considered myself a pessimist. Come to find out, I am actually an eternal optimist and a romantic at heart.

Who knew?

Andrew

Petals

A LOVE BOOK OF POEMS

A Flash of Light

Periodically I see a flicker in the corner of my eye
So bright I stagger backwards in surprise
I can't predict when it will come; it just happens
The power of the light shoots into my body
Warming me from the inside

I find myself constantly looking
Afraid to close my eyes, I don't want to miss it
So powerful, it scares me; so incredibly defined
But it's a good fear; I anticipate seeing it again
It comforts me
I believe it's a sign

A sign of what I do not know
but can't wait to find out
I think... if I really focus on it - it's a reminder to keep going
A reminder that as long as I keep fighting
good things will come
It's a clap; a strike from above
It is faith...it is hope... all rolled into one

As I look back on these moments something has occurred to me
The answer has been there all along
It's clear, I am no longer confused
The light; these intense flashes of peace I feel have one single source
For when I get them - when my heart skips a beat
I see my future
I see you

A New Man

I have been waiting for this fog to lift
  My mind to be clear
    For my thoughts to become my own again
      No more fear

You have opened up a door inside of me
  You have helped me breathe
    For the first time since I can remember
      My eyes have started to focus on something better
        I can finally see

That pressure that once crushed my chest has lifted
  I can take a breath
    The haunting images in my brain have gone away
      I can relax

The emptiness in my stomach has been filled
  I know where I belong
    The fear that once consumed me is gone
      Finally on the right track

You have done to me what no one else ever could
  You have shown me that life can be better
    Life can be good

A Shooting Star

I love to hear you laugh
When happiness is in your heart
To know what you have gone through; the obstacles you have faced
The thought of joy running through your body is music to my ears
Your smile glows brighter than a shooting star
If only for a moment the world finds balance
Love surrounds us all; no more tears

I love to listen to your voice
Harmony from above singing my favorite song
An aura of confidence slips off your tongue; your tone of compassion becomes a language only
angels can understand
Warmth rushes over me, like brushing your hand through the thin ocean sand

I love the kindness in your eyes
Behind them a mixture of light and depth I can't quite explain
A galaxy of beauty filled with the brightest bright you will ever see
The colors so incredibly perfect
They tell a story of an angel who is meant to fly in this world
Meant to be completely free

Most of all I love your inner core
Who you are on the inside; what you stand for
Everything about you is so kind and so pure
I can barely find the strength to look away
This perfection I am witness to, I am humbled you have chosen me
When you entered my life my world shook
I will never be the same

Above Average

Your feet shine in the warm sun
Like specs of gold in a mountain stream
Your legs, so smooth, remind me of drops of water
falling down the base of an icicle
I know you think of yourself as average
but you are anything but

When you enter a room heads turn your way
In a world where we talk without meaning
But when describing your beauty
I find myself with nothing to say

I get lost in your smile
    Your eyes take me to a desert island surrounded by the ocean breeze
        You move with strength and compassion gliding through the summer haze
      So graceful; like a dolphin playing in a choppy sea

I know you think you are average; normal compared to the rest
But they don't compare to you at all
You are a reminder to me of how love will always win
To me you are simply the best

Thank you for opening these doors in my life
    Thank you for walking through them with me
      Thank you for showing how to embrace love
        Thank you for showing me how "perfect" perfect can be

Best is Yet to Come

I know you feel stuck in the middle
Waiting for this ride to end
Feeling the weight of the world on your shoulders
Bending with the weight of other's decisions

It's not fair - you deserve better
Why this happened I will never know
But maybe with all of the pain
Better days are ahead
Feeling that appreciation for who you are; what you have
It's something only lessons in life can show

Keep fighting
Stay true to you and give yourself the love you deserve
Have faith this is just a new start
That sound you hear is a good thing; the beating in your chest
Wonderful things are ahead
Yes, the first part of your life was good
But the second half is going to be the best

Bodies Collide

I am working on it but it's hard for me
Learning to let go, learning to give in
My most recent loss still so fresh in my mind
      Almost forgot what it was like to win

I am cautious while looking at you
I have felt things that make me believe
Looking into your eyes I begin to dream
Feelings rush over me; I grab onto my courage and breathe a deep breath
      This feeling I must trust; need to discard the rest

I feel complete wrapped in your embrace
I can't let go not having experienced that before
Not two but one beating heart
This soul of mine released into your arms
      Thanks for opening that door

I know now what it means to share something deep; much deeper than oneself
To allow something in without holding back
For the very first time I have felt a part of something bigger than myself
      I have you to thank for that

Cautiously Optimistic

It's going to take years to get over
This betrayal I feel
Even though time has passed I find myself walking in a daze
This can't be real!

Emotionless - her face I don't recognize it anymore
Like someone has taken her place
It's like eating your favorite meal day after day
Then without notice everything changes - unrecognizable
no texture, no taste

I believe I deserve better
I've given it everything I've got
It's like my effort, my love, no longer matter
How can someone simply turn the switch?
No remorse, no consequence, no feeling, no thought
My faith in human nature has been shattered

All I have left now are pieces
So big I can barely pick them up
Still, while I struggle, I can no longer choose to be a victim
Enough is enough
Not sure what the future brings so I continue on
I will do it for the ones I love

I have failed before but in this case it's not an option
The sign is blinking in my heart and mind
The message printed in bold letters
Keep moving forward, but do so with caution

Close Your Eyes

Close your eyes...
Remember that time when you
were the happiest?
When you felt safe; completely secure
A time when life was a blessing
Everything surrounding you so
innocent and pure

Keep your eyes closed...
Feel now what you felt then
Let the warmth of love rush over you
Allow your heart to recognize that feeling of old
Reenergized by this gift of something new

I want you to know that my daily desire is to remind you of that each and every day
Now open your eyes...
Take my hand and let me show you the way

Pot of Gold

Everything so out of focus
A movie filled with black and white
I have seen this world through these shaded glasses for so long
It's funny how we sometimes deny ourselves the color of life
Even when we know things are wrong

Color can tell so many stories
Can define the edges of what you see
Help open your eyes in a way you have never seen before
Images flash in front of you like lightning in a humid evening's summer sky
So powerful, completely new
The reds, purples and blues consume you
Looking at this life of yours differently
Truly seeing for the very first time

Now that I have seen this new beauty I will never go back
Each day the colors change, but this time, they get brighter-
last longer
The blacks and grays I once knew seems like a
million miles away
I find myself staring at this rainbow; ready to follow it wherever it goes
These colors I see are coming from you
You are my pot of gold

Conflicted

Time sometimes goes so slow it feels like it's going backwards
I feel nervous as I watch it go by
It's like seeing something spectacular;
So overwhelmed with beauty yet I fear I'll never get to see it again
That's the best way to describe it
In awe of your smile, the feel of your skin

It's a power - a burst of energy
You can't see it but there's a connection between us;
An unbreakable rope connecting your soul and mine
It's love floating around us; inside of us
A presence you can't describe in words no matter how hard I try

I do feel guilty
Guilty that this connection didn't exist with people in my past
Sometimes I question if I had tried hard enough, if I truly gave love a chance
But maybe there's not an explanation
Maybe it's as simple as true love
Maybe this box was always locked inside of me and you have the key
Maybe it was simply meant to be

I do feel sad for those around me who can't experience this joy I feel
I've always put other people first
But then again, maybe this is our time
I won't apologize - I deserve to be happy too
My prayers were answered when God brought me you

Conquering the Mountain

This mountain I continue to climb is challenging
Full of jagged edges and steep terrain
I slip from time to time, rocks slippery from all the rain

While I can't turn around and go back I ask myself;
        Would I if I could?
                Yes at times it seems like an easier path but would that be best?
              Deep down I know the answer
                    Albeit hard, I keep climbing, I can't afford to rest

Ahead of me I see the peak of this mountain now within reach
I still have more climbing to do but I'm almost there
I look to my left and see you climbing beside me
Strength in your step, determination in your stare

You inspire me to keep fighting
        I hope I do the same for you
                One day we will reach the top together
              I pray it's someday soon

Until then, hand in hand, we will take this hill one step at a time
Trust me I won't let you slip
I am so blessed to have you as my climbing partner
I can't think of a better person to share this journey of mine

Dare to Dream

It's weird that I can be myself around you
Normally holding back; afraid
I've always wanted to be this person
Oh how I've prayed

I don't know where this is going
But I feel it's something more
Truthfully I don't think it's "just something new"
With you behind me I feel I can soar

I want to give you the strength you have given me
To help you get a sense of what I feel
I have been giving with little return for so long
The thought of someone accepting me is foreign-
can this be real?

Yes there is a long way to go
I don't know how this is going to end
While I continue with caution I am allowing myself to dream
To think "what if" for the first time
My companion
My lover
My very best friend

Day and Night

There are times when the worst part of my day is waking up and looking in the mirror
I can see how my thoughts while sleeping consumed me
Exhausted, looking lifeless at times

                                                                    My vision so foggy I can barely see

I think of revenge, I think of pain
Negativity fills my head
I don't like the person staring back; the person I have become
I can see the disappointment in my own eyes

                                                                    No words need to be said

I go about my day dazed and confused
But suddenly things begin to change
The pain starts to fade away the second I see you

As if I was sunbathing on the beach I soak up your sun
Guided by your light; your love changes me
Those evil thoughts I once felt disappear

                                                                    The pain begins to leave

The spring in my step carries me through the day
My smile begins to reappear
I start to enjoy life again
After feeling helpless, like a captain on a drifting ship

                                                                    I have power again, I can once again steer

Now I can look into the mirror at the end of the night
No longer troubled by the one staring back at me
Thanks to you I can finally sleep

                                                                    Happy with what I see

18

Final Resting Place

Have you ever watched a leaf float in the warm fall sky?
Pushed by the wind
If you watch long enough it will find its natural pace
It's final resting place

We all have a position in life
You just don't know it yet
The twists and turns of life lead the way
I don't know when or where my final resting place will be
Only certain that it will be upon me someday

Recently I have started to take a step back and look
This humbling ride has made some things clear
I'm trying to let go and accept my fate
Like watching the leaf; I try to appreciate the ride without being paralyzed by fear

Most of all, I have begun to appreciate the important people in my life more than ever before
Watching the leaf I realize, without wind, it will just stay there without any progress or flow
Thank you for being the wind in my life
Helping me get to where I need to go

Direct Connect

You are at a different level, beyond this place
  A place I can see but will never be able to understand
    A void between this world and the next
      A presence about you that literally stops time
        An angel who for some reason has chosen me
          A direct connection - God's vision and mine

When I was young, a world opened up inside of me
I recall a presence that pushed me towards opening up my heart to something greater than myself
It wasn't until I met this person face to face did I realize that this was the plan all along
One day she would find me
An open door to a realm I see but cannot completely describe
The light around her so amazingly strong

I sometimes get bogged down with this world of ours
  I focus on despair; the battle versus good and evil and everything in between
    But the truth is I have already witnessed a miracle that has given me hope
      I know there is something better for us all;
        another world beyond the one I can see
          You have shown me that
            I have now seen it - dreams do come true
              I know now that my dream from the very
                beginning was always you

Fingertips

When I run my hand over your forehead
My fingers glide like an eagle in the sky
Without direction, my senses overpowered by emotion
I look through your eyes and into your soul
Your breathing starts to change...my heart begins to fill
Time stands still
I feel like I can fly

The pads of my fingers try to remember every second
To hold onto the feel of your skin
Touching your face, almost scared to press too hard; to hurt this angel I see
I begin to shiver
My fingers, touching pure beauty, start to quiver

The simple things, while often overlooked, humble me to my core
I glide my fingers softly from your forehead to the back of your head
Moments too short yet so powerful, I fear they will end

If I was to describe seconds with you that's what I would say
Staring at an angel in front of me
Overwhelmed by her perfection

Ground Shake

I feel like I can stare directly into your soul
 I can see who you are; life running through your veins
  I see some broken pieces from your past
   Other times, cherished moments along the way
    The triumphs and challenges that have made you
     who you are today

I can almost feel the electricity in the air when you walk into the room
 The ground shifts ever so slightly
  I struggle to balance myself; to find my place
   Almost like I am experiencing love for the first
    time over and over again
     My heart begins to race

You see I am utterly amazed by you
 By the door you have opened in front of me and what's behind
  Overwhelmed - these words don't describe what I am feeling but I have to try
   Never before have I experienced something so powerful
    Magic becomes real
     My world slows down when you are near
      Just one of many descriptions of how I feel

Impact

Every morning I glance at the freshly filled sky

    It's a reminder of a new day
    I try to wipe the slate clean; forget about the mistakes from the day before
    I'm not perfect
    While I have lost some battles, I refuse to lose the war

It's a new day

    A new opportunity to make amends
    My motivation lies behind your strength
    Behind the innocence of your smile
    When I look at the morning sun I see your beauty in the rays; radiating for miles
    When I look at the clouds I see a magnificent masterpiece, color your eyes

You continue to be my compass

    You continue to push me to be better
    You keep the sound of conflict inside of me at a whisper instead of a roar
    While I don't tell you this nearly enough...
    I love you with all my heart
    The impact you have had on my life is something I will never ignore

Hands of Strength

My hands struggle to hold onto these obstacles in front of me
Worn out, blistering from overuse
The dry cuts stinging...
I feel the pain of reality with everything I do
Everything I see

My joints so slow and stiff as I grip these chains
I toss them aside
I do my best to block out this discomfort I feel
It does me no good to stop
Exhausted - I barely have the strength to kneel

     Keep fighting...

When I need it most, when I feel I can't take another step
I always seem to find a way
I look at the inspirations in my life; reminders to keep going no matter what
The images - the people I love fill my head
Standing up I dust off my pants and push ahead

All of a sudden the next mountain in front of me isn't as big as it looked before
I crack my knuckles and go to work; my hands still sore
While this cycle will repeat itself again and again, that I have no doubt; I know the things that truly matter will carry me through

     I will keep fighting...

I have to believe that in the end love will win out
My love for God, my love for others
My love for you

Hard to Measure

Have you ever loved someone so much the mere thought of something bad happening
makes you ill?
The intensity of how much you care makes your chest
want to burst?
Anything that is good in this world; anything that can happen that brings joy to this life
You want them to experience first

Think about how you would feel on your greatest day
Think about the happiness that would rush over your body like a tidal wave
so intense and completely free
Times that emotion by a million
Now you know what you mean to me

I would give anything to make sure even a simple smile is yours
I would move heaven and earth to make sure each day is better than the last
I would give my life for you without hesitation if given the chance

If you ever feel alone during this journey of yours
I want you to read this
Take the words in; know that you are special in every way
My love for you is as deep as the ocean
I promise never to let you down; to love you with
everything I have
every single day

Heart Attack

When I'm around you my heart moves at a different pace
Instead of a beat it connects with a pound
Every ounce of emotion pours into each strike
So intense it takes my breath away
Overwhelmed by this love I've found

I remember times in my life when the pieces were damaged
Trampled over; strewn about onto
the ground
They were walked on, kicked across the floor
Times when I questioned my self-worth
Felt like I couldn't take it anymore

Then you entered my life; everything changed
A smile replaced sadness, warmth replaced pain
I no longer have to look over my shoulder; watch where I walk
You have become my everything
My best friend
My role model
My rock

Hard to Wait

The pieces fit, it just takes time
Something I struggle with
I juggle this object with these hands of mine
Rolling it from one finger to the next
Trying to be as patient as I can
I know it will happen; I can almost see it developing
in front of me
Still, frustrated because I just don't know when

I would say my greatest weakness is my wandering mind
Searching for the faith I need; sometimes it's hard to find
Deep down I'm confident that my path will level off soon
These obstacles surrounding us will fade away
I can almost reach out and grab the future I see
I can't wait to love you in every single way
I pray....
Someday

My heart beats for you
My eyes recognize who you are
My ears will always be on guard for any cries of pain
My mind focused on your beauty as images of your smile occupy my mind

Most of all, the glow that surrounds you fills my soul
The light passes through your body and gives me hope
What are now radiant colors used to be a dull gray
Oh I can't wait to share my life with you...
It's coming I have to believe it
My dream will be reality someday

I Am Not Alone

If I had to choose between pain and fake
I'd choose pain
Between hurt and numb
I'd choose hurt
During those times of need we find out who we are
The people who love us make their presence known
This trying time helps me appreciate what I have
My loved ones with me on this journey
I am not alone

If I didn't feel the emotions of life
I wouldn't be able to see it
Recognizing the difference between make - believe and real
Love picks me up when I need it most; all of a sudden everything seems to fit
It's all around me
I close my eyes and take a deep breath
Love - that is what I feel

I'd Choose You

I wonder what life would be like if I had everything I ever wanted
If I exploded through daily challenges with ease
If money wasn't an issue, went around buying stuff as if it were free

I wonder what it would be like if I never felt fear
Never felt the sting of failure nor felt the tears of disbelief
I wonder if life was easy if I would ever appreciate the small victories
The touch of a loved one and what it means
The beautiful color blue of a mountain stream and everything beneath

The truth is I believe the answer would be no
In order to see kindness you must also see pain
In order to recognize love you must also feel loss
While life can be hard it can also be perfectly imperfect

Without those experiences I would never be able to
Appreciate what's fake and what's true
The light you bring to this world with everything you do
I know that if I had a choice to pick a world without feeling
Or a roller coaster journey that leads me to you...
I'd choose to walk this road one hundred percent of the time
If I had a choice, I would always choose you

I Promise

One of the hardest things I face is this helplessness I feel
Watching you...
I see life and its obstacles
I watch the pieces of the past fall to the ground
like shattered glass
I will do anything in this world to protect you
If you fall I will catch you
I will never let go
Nothing will ever break my grasp

People will try to break you down
They will try to control you
They will try to lock the door
It's a harsh reality that we both know all too well
They will try to keep you at their level
But know that you are destined for so much more

My promise to you is this...
I will be here from start to finish
I promise to always put you first
Instead of taking the wind away from you,
I vow to lift you with air
To fill your heart
To make it burst

32

Why Is It?

Why is it when I'm around you I breathe at a different pace?
Why is it that time slows down?
Why do the emotions inside of me rush through my body
like a runaway flood?
Speechless at times - all I hear are the words you say to
me;
No other sounds

Why do I focus on your eyes like a shooting star?
Constantly thinking about getting close to you just to
catch the smell of your scent
Why is my goal to make you laugh just to see your smile?
I close my eyes and focus
Hoping to hear the sound of your soul

Why is it that this power I have in front of me, at times, brings me to my knees
Standing still for so long I'm finally starting to believe
Perfection is a word used by many but only
experienced by a few
It's a word I never used or understood

That is until I met you

I Want You to Know

I want you to know I'm proud of you
Proud of the person you are
The person you are striving to be
I want you to know that everything you do, everything you are
It inspires people who know you
You inspire me

Don't let the noise derail you
The ones who put themselves first - don't pay attention to their voice
They have chosen to put greed in front of love, themselves in front of others
They alone made that choice

I want you to know that this isn't about me
While I cherish my days with you by my side,
your happiness comes first above everything else
These words I believe in with all my heart
I'm so incredibly proud of the person you are
I'm honored to know you
       Your strength
              Your integrity
                     Your courage
The qualities you possess will ALWAYS set you apart

I Will Give You

I don't know when the clouds will clear, but I promise they will
I don't know when the rain will stop, but the sun will shine again soon
I don't know when you will feel completely free but
I promise that day is coming
Be patient - trust in me
Let me help you

If the words don't convince you, look into my eyes
You will see what you mean to me
You will see the respect I have for you;
for the person you have come to be
Through my eyes I ask you to believe

I will never be perfect, but I promise to give you perfect effort
I promise to support you in every way
If you have ever wondered what it would be like
to be treated like a queen
Let me show you...
I promise to shower you with love each and every day

I will give you my everything
I will give you my soul
I will give you my identity
My heart is full

I Will Protect You

This is how I see you my love....

I lie here and wonder what it all means
    My thoughts are my only company
        Overwhelmed I can't sleep - can't even rest
            The only peace is knowing that I'm doing my best

Working so hard to protect everyone else
I don't have time to think about me
I see the pain on the faces of people I love
Sometimes I just feel so empty

The ones close to me though remind me of this
    I didn't make this choice
        Looking at these puzzle pieces, I'm trying to put them together
            Every decision is made with one goal -
                trying to make things better

I don't know what to do
I'm guided by faith, the driver is my heart
Keeping my family safe is where I start

It's a lot to take on, there is no doubt
    But without knowing it I've been preparing my entire life
        I've always been my family's rock
            As a mom and as a wife

God challenges us in life but never more than we can take
I will continue to lead. Come my children I will protect you.
As long as we are together we will succeed

Imprint

I can't see you but I know you're there
The energy around me changes
A wave of peace rushes over me without warning
A small smile creeps onto my face out of nowhere as a familiar warmth fills the air

Thank you for those moments I desperately need
I still feel so lost; missing you beyond belief
It's your presence... that light that sheds off of you that I take with me everywhere I go
From the day I first met you - *the real you* - you have been seared into my soul

Even when I'm not with you, you are always there
Inside my skin
Inside my lips
Inside my body
Every corner of every part
You control the deepest depths of who I am
You control my heart

Teaching Moments

I can see the courage behind your eyes
I know the strength you have inside
I'm amazed as I watch your spirit speak in front of me
Challenges that would cripple most, you simply take a deep breath and let out a sigh

While I'm honored to share this journey with you
Inspired by every moment watching you fight
I'm also struggling; knowing you are experiencing such pain
I want to take it away from you, but I can't
It's not fair
It's just not right

I get angry
Often times I am sad
But I can't let my emotions take control of me
If I do I'm afraid I'll miss the lessons you continue to teach
Bravery... Integrity... A passion for life... The compassion you give
You continue to show me how to love
You continue to show me how to live

Inspiring Me

If there is one thing that defines you it's your strength
It may not mean much now; not to you
But you inspire me and so many others
It's a trait coveted by so many, yet shared by a few

Next is your compassion
Your heart pure as the summer sky
Never question the integrity of your emotions
No matter how many times you ask why

But most of all is your dedication
To the people you love and the ones close to you
You see that's what truly sets you apart
I believe God has put you into a position to make a difference
It's time that you believe that too

Life Line

Across the board, when asked about what they love most,
every astronaut talks about the beauty of space
The overwhelming feeling of how small we truly are in this magnificent place

The one fear they share is the thought of losing their grip
And floating away without control
Only held onto by a life-line that keeps them grounded,
brings stability to their body; their soul

The description of space can also be used in life
We are just specks in this overall masterpiece, trying to find our way
I want you to know that if you lose your grip,
like the astronaut in space, and feel like you have lost control
        I will grab you
                I will protect you
                        I won't let go

Love Again

I don't want to tell her yet - It's just not the right time
Besides I don't think she would believe me
I remember feeling something special; something different the first time we met
Almost immediately inspired to become the person I was meant to be

Cautious I move forward
Trying not to scare her away
Knowing these feelings I have are strong
Every inch of my soul believes we will be together someday

It's hard to explain how I got to this point yet I know this is where I belong
Some might question my motive, how can I be here?
To start, her smile is warm and her heart is pure
Her strength and her character set her apart
Perfect in every way, yet not afraid to admit her fears

Laughter and compassion
Something as simple as the smell of her hair
Her flame for life is contagious
This total package of beauty, inside of out, is extremely rare
I thought I knew what love was once before
I have always been searching for my soulmate
Now, dreaming of my future with her makes me realize my wait is over
It's hard to sit still
I can hardly wait

Someday I hope she realizes what these words of mine truly mean
How thanks to her I feel whole again
For the first time since I can remember
I'm focused on where I'm going, instead of where I've been

Making Sense

I couldn't put my finger on it for the longest time
I knew it was there; just didn't know how to find it
It seems all I could do was continue to fight
Almost like a fishing line in the water - searching...
Waiting for a bite

The simple struggles confused me the most
It was always so hard yet seemed easy in my mind
The person across from me was supposed to understand what I was
I guess the fact that I always felt like second best should have been my first sign

Now that I have some distance from that life
I am starting to see
See that no matter how hard I tried
It just wasn't meant to be
Now, every day it seems, I am learning something new
It's not a coincidence that my world started to change for the better the day I found you

I promise to show you every day how much I appreciate your presence
The way you have changed me for the better in every way
Thanks to you I no longer have to try to figure out what was missing
With the ultimate partner by my side, I am no longer afraid

Me Being Me

Please understand that when you feel pleasure, so do I
    When you are relaxed, I feel at peace
        When you smile, my worry melts away
            When I am able to show you my appreciation, I feel complete

When you enter the room, I will open the door
    When you sleep, I will give you exhilarating dreams
        When you fall, I will pick you up
            When you are tired and can barely stand, you can lean on me

I know you struggle with this idea
    The idea of me devoting everything I have to you each and every day
        You want to give me the attention I give you
            But by allowing me to show you my love; giving you everything I have
            You are giving me everything I want, everything I need
            By letting me do that for you
            You're letting me
            Be me

Mermaid

Drowning; running out of air
Surrounded by darkness - fading fast
I try to swim to the surface but I can't
Being dragged to the bottom by these chains of my past

I look up, struggling to break free
Ready to concede
All of a sudden a figure appears in front of me
She glides toward me - glowing; so bright she lights up the sea
As she approaches, I am able to see that she has something in her hand
Just when I needed it most, she brings me a key

She takes off the shackles; I'm finally free
Truthfully free for the very first time
She takes my hand and pulls me to safety
At the surface, I can breathe

Thank you for finding me
Thank you for saving me when you did

Midnight Sky

At night I often find myself watching the stars
A world of imagination with endless possibilities
I can't help but think of what's behind the curtain;
how can so much beauty exist in one place?
A shooting star streaks across the sky

                                        A feeling of warmth rushes over me

At that moment it's like God is beside you sharing his plan
You get lost in the silence of the night, yet the energy surrounding you has a voice
For a second you feel as though you have found your place
You are exactly where you are supposed to be
The knots inside of you come apart

                                        You feel overwhelmingly free

I want you to know that the feeling I describe
also applies to you
Every time I look into your eyes or caress your hair
It's the same type of appreciation that consumes me;
just like the midnight sky on a clear summer night
Like those times I have found myself gazing at the stars with God by my side
In your presence, I am completely at peace
The world makes sense

                                        Everything feels right

My Pledge

My pledge is to always put you first
To think of you before myself
To cherish your gifts without expectation
Honor the person you are above everything else

My pledge is to thank you when you don't expect it
To hug you when you need it most
Stand by you when life attacks
No matter the challenge, to see it through
Wrap my arms around your heart
I will protect you

My pledge is to hold your hand through this journey
At times walking side by side, other times in front or behind you
Your hand never too hot or too cold for my grip
To support you in every way possible
Especially the days when you don't think you can continue

My pledge above all else is to love you for the rest of my life and beyond
To never betray the trust we share
I pledge to show you that this power we have built together will last forever
A bond so perfect; a bond so rare

My Premonition

I once had a dream that shook me to my core
It felt so incredibly real
To this day I can replay it in my mind; it ended too soon
It came at a time in my life when I needed it most
Helped me begin to heal

On one end of the room was me
Struggling through the pressures of life
Looking for direction; my face filled with pain
The other side of the room was also me, but this version was better
I was at peace
Back and forth the two talked about life - the internal conflict we feel
The battle between acceptance and disappointment
The overwhelming power of the beast

Through the conversation came understanding
The better of the two shouted words of encouragement and words of strength
The better me discussed the power of life; the power of faith

Before the dream came to a close, before I opened my eyes
The better of the two me's said something I will never forget
A Prediction I will never get out of my head
He said 'be patient as the gift you seek is coming
When she finds you your world will become complete
She will give you the meaning you seek.'

For years I have been waiting
Praying those words would someday become true
As I sit here now I realize that the dream I speak of wasn't a dream at all
It was a message directly from above for it was an angel I was speaking to
The angel was referring to you

My Search is Not Over

I remember when I was young
I had a dream about who I wanted to be
As the moments rushed by I started to lose myself
from time to time
Looking back on things now it's so easy to see

I still remember how I once felt
That inner search will never go away
Finding someone to share my life with
Experiencing unconditional love each and every day

It's not easy to describe it
Written words always seem to fall short
My heart has bled and continues to bleed
My expectations about life, while sometimes too high,
continue to haunt me
My body overflowing with love
Sharing that journey with my soulmate
Something I desperately need

I hear stories of life partners growing old, hand in hand;
more in love with one another now than ever before
Inspired by the thought of true love winning out
I think back to the person I once knew
It's never too late, and with you in my life, just maybe
Just maybe that dream I once had might come true

My Waterfall

Take this pain - I don't want it anymore
I want to feel free
I am ready for this waterfall to wash me clean
I am ready to once again be me

I have struggled more than most
This journey has taken its toll
I have paid my dues
I'm ready to take a different road

While my past will always be a part of who I am
The memories will never fade
I will no longer let them define me

I'm ready to jump into this water and let it take me away
Ride it downstream to something new
Let the stream wash away these scars - cleanse my heart
Feel the clean water wash over me
Looking forward to a fresh start

Needle and Thread

It started with a needle and thread
A steady hand
A patient stroke up and down, side to side
Meticulously paying attention to every detail
Slowly the rips came together; the holes began to fill
The power of your hands brought everything together
Your masterpiece was done
What was once several different pieces
All of a sudden become one

With the flick of your wrist you changed everything
Stitches made out of love
What was once pain is hope
You made everything better
I want to thank you for giving me
the greatest gift I could ever ask for
Thank you for sewing my heart back together
again

Never Alone

Every time you cry a piece of me dies
Every speck of sadness in your eyes brings me to my knees
I shudder at the thought of you in pain
Like a punch to my stomach I can hardly breathe

I'm your protector yet I can't shield you from this
I'm sorry to admit it out loud
I will however be there to help you
Pick you up if you fall to the ground

I am so frustrated when I think of life treating you this way
It's time for someone else to take over
You have been through enough with nothing more to prove
Until then know that as you continue to walk this road you will never walk it alone
Now and forever I'll be there walking right beside you

New Shoes of Mine

I'm so sick of these shoes I've been wearing
They just don't fit
Truth is I've known that for a while now; the pain they have caused me
This burden I have been wearing for so long
I ask myself why now?
I know the answer
No matter how hard they were to wear I just didn't want to quit

I'm finally untying the laces, my feet can finally breathe
The wounds from my time with them on will eventually heal
As I take them off, my legs are as light as air
A gigantic relief rushes over me
No longer tied to this weight of mine
I finally feel free

For the first time I am finding myself
Trying on a different pair of shoes
Ones that fit me better; feel secure
They allow me to scale mountains with a single leap
I am walking differently now
I'm allowed to be me

The best way I can describe these new shoes of mine is that I don't feel like I'm wearing any at all
They are perfect in every way
Once grounded, I'm floating
I'm looking down on this new life; so incredibly high in the sky
After walking for so many years
With these new shoes of mine I can finally fly

Passing Through

As I sit here I can feel a stirring inside
A mixture of impatience and excitement
Fear and anxiousness all rolled into one
I wish I could blink my eyes and the future I see
would be right here in front of me

It's a harsh reminder of what I've gone through, but also a victory of the human spirit
How someone can affect things so drastically
How one person can clear the fog with a single breath
The power of love that I once thought failed me has rushed back
like a vengeance to help me see
Rescued me when it seemed I had nothing left

All of a sudden I have this presence in my life more powerful than what I have experienced before
I am humbled - I find myself weak at the knees
In awe of this experience my goal as I move forward is to cherish every moment I have left
No longer walking, I find myself running with excitement as I pass though this open door

On the other side of that door I see you...
I see us together at last

Overwhelmingly Humble

A glowing figure in the dark of a room
The brightest bright
Being able to see for the very first time
The gift of sight
The overwhelming feeling of love spreading
across the room
All things that can only be described as
perfectly beautiful
That's exactly what I feel when I see your face
How I describe you

I have told you before that I am scared
Scared that this gift is too good to be true
I don't deserve this angel
What have I done to deserve this?
What have I done to deserve you?

You are who I think of when I wake up and
when I go to sleep
You are who I think of during those
moments in between
I am honored to receive this gift and will cherish it every second of the day
Each day I promise to repay you for what
you have given me
Somehow
Some way

Perspectives

I often think about the people in my life
How some have embraced me in life while others
have given me pain
Some have taken advantage of the person I am
Others have invited me in without motive or personal gain

I don't take this journey lightly
I am often disappointed with what I find
But with all of the defeats, every once in a while I come across someone who makes up for it
Someone who changes the game

I could sit here and wonder
Dwell on what was and what could have been
Instead, I choose to appreciate this gift
An angel that appeared when I needed it most
Once grounded in life by concrete
Now free; humbled by this divine shift
Thank you for showing me this loving perspective

Picture Perfect

It started with a kiss
A well-timed peck on the cheek
It set me free
I began to imagine the possibilities
  Before I knew it, what I was looking for was right there standing in front of me

Very few can relate to this life we share
To this bond that was created one brick at a time
Soulmates now but best friends first
Having a partner by my side who matches my passion for life
Laughter that fills the air
  Utterly and completely in love with this love of mine

It started with a kiss...
The flirtatious talk of a ring...
Mother nature's fireworks that shook the trees
What followed has been the best years of my life - a perfect dream
Your smile provided me a key that opened up a door
A gateway to another world that has left me speechless
It has taken over my soul
The only thing that has changed from then 'til now is
how I feel about you
I loved you then
  And today, I love you even more

Proof

I have been hurt before
It's hard for me to relax
This light that has surrounded me now is pure no doubt
Still, I can't help looking over my shoulder from time to time
After all, I have felt secure before - like everything was fine

But here's the thing...
What I am feeling now is different than the past
I think for the first time I have found what I've been looking for
It scares me; sometimes I question if this reality is true
The more I learn the stronger my love grows;
but what if I lose this one too?

I do worry about that at times
However, when I do, I find myself looking into your eyes
Like a flash, calmness rushes over me with what I see
That uncertainty I felt a moment ago - once so powerful, begins to subside

I have known distrust before
I have felt my heart break in two
You have stitched it back together, made me whole again
Like I'm brand new

Once controlled by fear, I can finally start to plan without
that voice inside of head
Trying not to be afraid of this gift; something so new
I can finally be me again
That's truly how I know at the end of the day this is meant to be
My proof is the love I feel for you

Queen of My Castle

This castle I build around you is built with stone
Each crack filled, no air will get through
The roof so sturdy it will support the highest winds

                                                                    Don't worry my love I won't let anything in

On guard I scan the horizon
At the ready; I will battle whatever threatens to cause harm
If ever a challenge comes knocking, asking your name
I will step in front of the storm without hesitation

                                                                        I'll wrap you in my arms

I vow not to let pain sting you without warning
Not to let the rain block out your sun
When you feel alone in your darkest times,
I will take your hand

                                                                    We will become one

This is a promise I give to you
With this castle I have built
I will protect you 'till my very last breath
My mission is clear; now and forever
You are my queen - I will give everything I have for you

                                                                I will fight until there's nothing left

Rainbow

I remember watching the storm clouds approach
The sky was the darkest dark
The intensity of the wind shook me to my core
It was something I had never seen before

When the storm hit I did my best to hold on
Helpless - I stood there getting pelted by the hail and rain
The thunder and lightning was so intense I questioned whether or not I would make it through
I remember how broken I felt
I'll never forget the pain

But here's the thing...
When the storm finally moved past me - despite being dazed and confused
I looked to the sky and saw a rainbow that took my breath away
I stared at it for the longest time;
Just standing there in awe with nothing to say
I can't quite explain it but it gave me the peace I had been searching for
It was so beautiful; so true
Soon I realized that everything would be okay
Because that rainbow was like looking at you

Ready for Anything

I can see a storm brewing in the distance
The waves building; the changing tides
Clouds darkening, lightning strikes filling the sky
It's almost like the entire horizon is moving in your direction all at once
So powerful, yet beautiful at the same time
I find myself just standing there - I can't believe my eyes

But I am not afraid

I have you standing next to me
Holding your hand I feel your strength
As long as we are together, I know what we can overcome - how much we can take

As the storm approaches...
As the wind begins to blow and the water begins to rise

I stand my ground

I squeeze your hand and glance into your eyes

I'm ready for anything

I know there is nothing I can't handle as long as I have you by my side

Ready for Battle

Life gets away from us sometimes
It takes its toll
Watching things happen all around us
Feeling out of control

Those are the times when I want
you to step aside;
Don't get bogged down - don't run
I am standing beside you
Here I come

Allow my love to shield you from all
of the pain you see
I will go to battle for you with
everything I have
Take my hand; follow me

Let me set you free

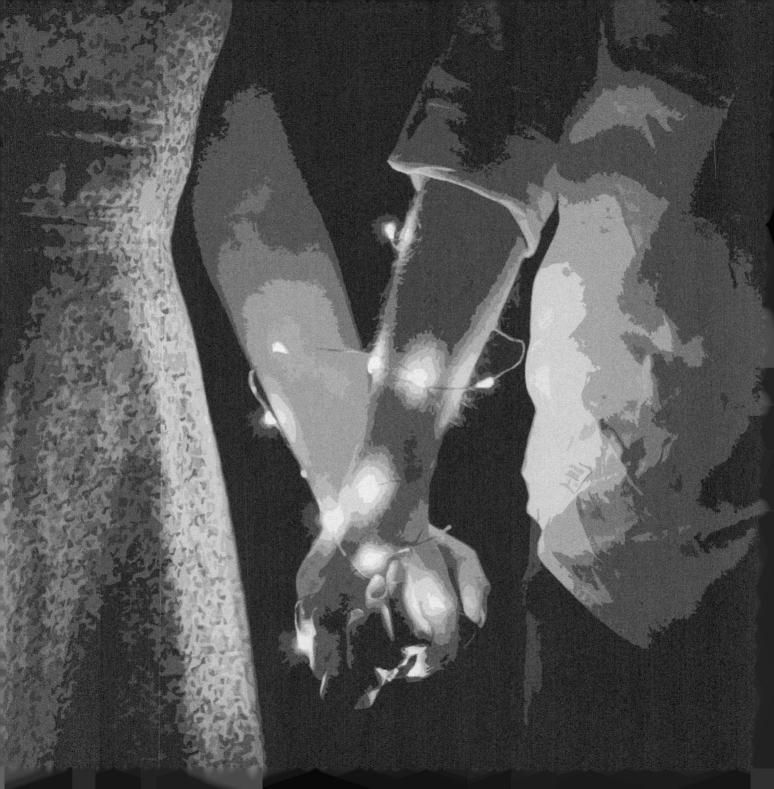

Security

I walk into these rooms and I feel eyes focus on me
    My skin begins to tighten; my heart starts to pound
        In my mind it feels like everything stops
            No more talking, no more sound

I don't know why I feel this way
    It's not my cross to bear
        Still I walk with pieces of disappointment falling from me
            I want to scream; just make it go away
                It doesn't feel fair

But at the same time it makes me appreciate you even more
    No matter how I felt before, the sight of your smile seems to make it go away
        I talk about being your protector but the truth is you are mine
            Like a cocoon, the strength around you wraps me up; I feel secure
                No matter how difficult the storm you help me manage the fear

Thank you

Scream and Shout

I want to scream out loud
Shout at the top of my lungs to everyone I know
I want to announce it to the world
Look each and every person in the eye

Tell them about the love I feel inside
How my heart is ready to explode

I want to cry tears of joy
Jump up and down; raise my hands in the air
I want those around me to stop and listen

To put down what they are doing
Listen and stare

I want everyone to hear what it's like to feel your love
To see the affect it has on me - how it has given me meaning in everything I do
This gift is overwhelming - I can barely take it all in
My soul now sings this perfect tune

My heart beats a perfect beat
It's all because of you

Snow Shovel

Life can be like a snowstorm at times
Freshly fallen – building onto the previous pieces from the past
That is if you decide not to push the debris aside,
Toss it away when you have the chance
Snow keeps piling
The weight of the shovel more challenging than it was before
      Building... until you can't take it anymore

You amaze me for so many reasons but how you embrace the storm sets you apart
Never afraid of the finish, always focused on the start
Life scares some; disables others
Watching you plow through the drifts, with a shovel in hand, motivates them - it motivates me
      You are my role model
      You are who I aspire to be

Someday Soon

It pains me to think about it
Seconds drag, they feel like years
The air becomes thick; hard to breathe
Struggling with everything I do
My mind consumed by the picture of your smile
The days roll by without meaning when I'm without you

It's not that I can't function
It's just different when you are here
The sights and sounds around me are clear
The beauty more defined
It becomes easier for me to find meaning in this life of mine

I can hardly wait for the days when this future becomes clear
When I can witness your greatness every day;
join hands with you and enjoy the ride
When that day comes I promise to enjoy every moment
Every single second with you by my side

Soul Begins to Sing

What does it mean to be happy?
    Can you describe it?
        Waves of feelings rushing over you like an ocean
          Like a thousand butterflies inside of your stomach
          Standing there frozen like a statue
            While everything around you is in motion

I close my eyes trying to find the words
    Every part of me taking it all in
      I can feel tiny tingles of laughter rushing through me
       Concentrating on each moment so I don't miss a thing
        My heart pounds - I listen closely; my soul begins to sing

A smile comes to my face
    A warmth surrounds my inner core
      The words I struggle to find never do come
      I think of you
        That's the definition I've been trying to find but can't explain

Simply put, words will never be able to describe something so pure - something so true

Speaking from Experience

I want you to know this feeling isn't going to last
       I want you to know you are not alone
              We go through life experiencing bumps along the way
                     When they happen, the important people in your life surround you
It will be okay

I want you to know that this darkness won't last
       I want you to know there is a plan
              Despite the pain, time will help this wound heal
                 Be patient - trust in God, he is your biggest fan

I want you to know that these words aren't just words at all
       I have been where you stand today
             Hopeless at times, I somehow made it;
             I found my way

Lean on me and the ones you love for we are here, ready to help you through
       Take my hand I am here to fight this battle with you

Static Electricity

I play it over and over in my head
My fingertips gripping the sensors on your skin
Starting with the back of your neck- I close my eyes
I try to hold onto this feeling rushing over me deep inside

I slide down your neck to your shoulder blades
Your skin so soft it's like my fingers have skates, sliding on ice
I try to soak up every inch of who you are
My finger strokes follow the groove of your back down your spine
Focused - determined not to miss a moment;
I find myself getting lost in time

I move my fingers to the middle of your back
So smooth, I can almost talk to your muscles along the way
My touch thanks them for allowing me a glimpse of perfection
Skin so smooth like a velvet sheet; glistening like newly fallen rain on the ground
Time slows to a snail's pace - the world fades away
No more sound

I reach the bottom of your back
The curves of your hips define my path
Your skin spreads out like a wave in the ocean
The heat from the friction shoots up my arm, travels to my soul
I find my fingertips wanting more
I bring my hand back to the base of your neck and do it again
A spiritual journey I can't describe
Something I've never felt before

Stitches

If you look close enough the evidence is there
        Cuts that have been stitched, the scars remain
They cannot be erased - cannot be repaired

I find myself looking at life differently now
        Cautious of what's coming next
                I scan the room unable to relax
        I rub my eyes trying to forget about the pain
These stitches remind me no matter where I go the heartbreak could return

It's a long journey and I'm not sure when I will be totally free
        But you have started to show me scars aren't always bad
                While they remind me of the past, they also drive me towards what I deserve
                        I run my hands over where these stitches once were
                They are healed now...
        I reflect on my journey with time as my teacher
With your help, amazed at what I've learned

Suit of Armor

Let me spend the rest of my days opening up doors
That were once in your way
Let me remove the weight from your shoulders; lift you up
Chisel away at this road in front of you
Make it smooth - remove the bumps

If you ever find yourself stuck in quicksand I will give you a rope
Whenever you feel stranded; treading water in the middle of the ocean I will bring you a boat
If ever scared to take on new challenges
I will help you try
Stuck on top of a mountain afraid to jump I will leap off with you
Together we can fly

I promise to spend the rest of my days protecting you
You will never fall - I am your parachute
My hope is that the greatest things life has in store rushes your way
That the happiness will overwhelm you; make you burst
Anything present meant to cause you harm will not succeed
For it will have to go through me first

Sunset

I am at peace
My feet swallowed up by the sand
The cool rush of the water behind it shoots up my spine
Lost only in the moment, consumed by the ocean air
I look at the perfect image of your silhouette glistening from the power of the sun
In awe how I feel complete knowing you are there

                    A love I've never felt before
                    Overwhelmed... completely in awe

I am confident now more than ever that you are a gift from God
An angel from above sent to save me
To enlighten me...
To inspire me...
Once lost; walking the wrong road
Your presence has adjusted my course
Helped me find me

                    The person I was meant to be
                    My destiny

I'll admit I have a hard time letting go
Fear of a future without you by my side paralyzes me from the inside
I know life can change - it moves like the ocean tide
But then I close my eyes and feel the sand
Embracing the water as it washes the worries away
I know love like this will never leave
Like the horizon during a sunset off the coast
It will travel on for eternity
I never witnessed a miracle until I met you

                    Now I see
                    You are here for me

Take my Hand

I find myself constantly watching you
    In awe of what you represent
        Frankly it makes me want to be better
            Own the words I've spoken, the actions I've meant

Your strength pours out of your body
    Like snow from a winter sky
        Mesmerized I thank God for your presence
            In a trance as time rushes by

Please know now that in this time of need
    While you feel alone I am rallying behind you
        While this pain feels like it won't go away
            I will help you paint this canvas new

Lean on me now for I will protect you
    Lay your head on my chest
        Now it's my turn to give you the strength you have given me
            I will not fail you
                I have learned from the best

Taking Notes

I watch you across the room
You smile and it becomes increasingly clear
You are different from the rest
Your heart is pure

I take notes as I go
Watching your every move; your perfection overwhelms me
Inspired by your lead I find myself wanting more
Through this darkness I once focused on; things are starting
to change for me
I'm finally starting to see

The power of the heart for some is earth-shattering
Like an earthquake putting a crack in the ground
I find myself wanting to be so much better because of you
Each day challenged by this inspiration I've found

Thank you for showing me the way when I needed it most
For helping me repair myself; to once again become whole
Your gift of love and compassion has brought me back to life
Once so empty; your actions have repaired my heart

And my
soul

The Oak Tree

We come from different backgrounds
Different families, different experiences
We are different roots feeding the same tree
With that, we also share the same goal
We are dedicated to each other
I complete you and you complete me

Like the lifelines of a mighty redwood
If one root fails the rest of the tree will suffer
The key to a strong base - strong enough to withstand the highest winds -
is all of the moving parts working together
Working in unison

We may have come from different places
But now our journey has collided;
brought together by a power from above
Working together I promise to help make the base of this tree stronger than the strongest oak
Nothing will be able to penetrate the shell surrounding this trunk
Not when our tree is built with respect and love

The Best I Can Do

Imagine being blindfolded, desperately wanting to see
You hear sounds around you, things you recognize but you cannot get a glimpse
The desire to look at everything in front of you grows deep inside
So much beauty

You feel like you want to explode
Emotions so strong; they won't subside

Imagine not being able to say what you want to the person you love
Almost like duct tape over your mouth
The words are on the tip of your tongue
You scream inside but nothing comes out

The butterflies stir deep inside,
your emotions run like a runaway flood

Have you ever seen something so beautiful?
Speechless - you almost have to shield your eyes
You know how you feel inside but you can't find the words to explain it

Words don't exist; you can't describe it
No matter how hard you try

If only for a second, the world slows down
Everything around you stands still
You feel safe; secure with where you fit in this journey called life
You have been here before; still, it always feels like the very first time
It feels new

This is the best way I can describe it
When I describe how it feels to make love to you

The Little Things

What makes you different from the rest are the little things
Diamonds of life that too many times go unnoticed - get lost with all of the noise
A helpful hand, a caring word when you need it most
The ability to handle adversity with class and poise

In the past, when the big events happened, at times someone was there
but it was often few and far between
However life is full of hiccups that need attention whether big or small
It's the little things that matter most
Determine a relationship's success whether it will rise or fall

I have noticed that with you, the little things bear the most weight
Small actions; simple truths that don't require explanation
Puzzle pieces that I could never find before
While still cautious, it makes me believe this wave I've been riding for so long
May finally find a shore

There are so many little things I admire about you
So many reasons why you are always in my thoughts
Thank you for helping me complete this puzzle
For helping me connect the dots

The Road to Happiness

I often think about the complexity of life
Why some periods of our journey seem easy while others are not
How the road we are on at times seems smooth while other paths lead to nowhere at all
They simply just stop

How we find our way varies, but the goal is always the same
We want to find where we belong in this world
Once we get there we desperately want to stay

I know that when it comes to my journey, while I am certainly not done
I feel I have started to find my road
The pavement is leveling off
I seem to have found stable ground just when I needed it most
Thanks to you, I feel I have found my map - found my rock

While the complexities of life will never go away
With you by my side it seems different
For the first time since I can remember I'm not afraid of where this road will lead
You have inspired me to keep driving
Your presence in my life has brought out the best in me

Through My Eyes

I'm more patient with you by my side
More relaxed, more in touch with me
The weight that once pressed on my chest has lifted
I can finally breathe

I find myself recognizing the little things more
    The importance of the simplest actions
        An offer to help, a small act of love
            You make me feel at peace with myself; the world around me
              I feel hope with the plan set forth from above

When you are struck by the selfishness in this world
That others have brought to your doorstep
Know that you are loved by so many
Appreciated for the person you are
You are the light from the sun that warms us all
You are the sparkles of light coming off a calm lake during a full moon
In a sky filled with the brightest objects one could ever see;
You are my shooting star
The best of the best - who we all should be aiming to be

    Remember that... Always

Today Is Our Day

Today is our day
A moment when we take the next step
I commit to you; you commit to me
Our days as individuals are done
Today we commit to each other; we finally become one

These vows cannot be taken lightly
They will be challenged during good times and bad
We will flourish; we will struggle
We will laugh, we will cry
No matter what, we need to remember that at the end of the day
We are a team, you and I

Anyone can pledge commitment to something when momentum is on your side
But what separates pretend from true love is a partnership that withstands it all
Yes, today is our day- let's enjoy it
Still... this is just the start
Remember we are in this together for the rest of our lives

Til' death do us part

Together

I am sitting here shaking
I know what needs to be done
Just for a second, my instinct is to run

Some people are challenged more than others
It's a basic fact of life
I have learned that God expects more from me than most
While others may cower, I choose to fight

I grab the hand of the person next to me and take a deep breath
Not sure what's going to happen only that I'm doing my best
My family, friends and God gather around me
I can feel their strength and they feel mine
Together we will defeat this darkness
Someday soon the sun will once again shine

Trusting What You Hear

The noise is all around us
If we let it, it will consume who we are
Before we know it we lose sight of where we are going; where we want to be
It dims the light surrounding our destiny star

Life is noisy
I struggle to decipher the static I hear
What messages are there to help me
What messages are generated by fear

How do we make our way through this noise?
When will the sound let me be?
I believe the answer lies deep within our soul
I focus - challenging the different voices coming from deep inside of me

Sometimes the noise around us is so loud
The strength of it; so deafening my heart blisters
But I am figuring something out during this journey of mine, as I peel away the crust
The screaming I hear is from the ones who are trying to lead me astray
What we need to listen to are the whispers from the people we trust

Walk With Me

Frustrated...
Each day passes with the same feeling of confusion
Anxiety attacking your inner core
The feeling so overwhelming, at times beyond despair
You desperately want to belong...
Somewhere
I know where you are
I've been there

Here's what I've learned
You are not alone despite how you feel
Even though you want to change; don't
You are the person you are, the person you were meant to be
Come to accept yourself
Love yourself
Let the feeling of peace rush over you
Stop listening to the demons of the past
It's time you let them go free

Easier said than done but that doesn't mean it can't happen
Start slow, small steps that will eventually turn into a run
I pray that one day you will get to where you are meant to go
That one day the darkness you see fades and is replaced by the sun

I am praying for you...
For answers to the questions you have
For the weight you feel to one day lift away
My hope is that reading this brings peace to your soul - it brightens your day
That the smile on your face is here to stay

What is Beautiful?

It means someone who knows oneself but is dedicated to others
One who expresses oneself not just by voice but also in touch

Someone whose smile lights up the day
One whose power is shown with random acts of kindness and compassion
Expressed by personal connections
Just as powerful as the words they say

More than anything, beautiful is the heart one keeps
and the wisdom of their soul
You, my friend, define beauty
You, my love, are beautiful

What's Important

Without consciously knowing it I have certain dates that control me
Periods in my life where plans have changed without warning; marked by pain
I find myself looking at the calendar, dreading the dates as they approach
Putting more stock in the ones surrounded by darkness
Instead of the times in my journey filled with light

Looking at it from the outside I'm cheating myself
I'm giving things outside of my control more attention than they deserve
Those periods of time in my life have taken enough from me already
It's time I treat those dates like just another day and move forward with what I've learned

I vow from this point forward to focus on the anniversaries marked with love and hope
Focus on memories that fill my heart with joy - days that bring a smile to my face
Thankful for what I have instead of what I don't
Blessed with the love I have for myself

The love for others
My love for you
Those are the things I choose to embrace

What is your heart telling you?

_____

_____

_____

_____

_____

_____

_____

_____

_____

_____

_____

_____

Photo Credits

Front/Back Cover – www.pexels.com/photo/three-red-roses-near-red-box-776649/

Page 6 – www.pexels.com/photo/happy-couple-walking-on-a-field-4545868/

Page 15 – www.pexels.com/photo/photography-of-a-woman-lying-on-flowers-813968/

Page 21 – www.pexels.com/photo/hugging-couple-beside-seashore-1463563/

Page 24 – www.pexels.com/photo/couple-hugging-each-other-3371269/

Page 43 – www.pexels.com/photo/person-facing-sideways-outdoors-2783151/

Page 54 – www.pexels.com/photo/unknown-person-standing-outdoors-2379179/

Page 62 - www.pexels.com/photo/man-and-woman-holding-each-others-hand-wrapped-with-string-lights-792777/

Page 80 – www.pexels.com/photo/adult-affection-bed-closeness-414032/

Page 11/28/37/61/86 –Vector rose – www.pixabay.com/vectors/encouraging-floral-flower-flowers-2023283/

For more information on the author and additional poems,

log onto http://www.telatype.com

Made in the USA
Middletown, DE
09 February 2022

60897698R00057